Presidents of the USA

From Washington to Obama

By Jack Lexington

Contents

Introduction

Thank you for choosing my book. Inside there will be facts about all of the US presidents in order, aswell as some myths about a number of the Presidents. Obviously as I say in order, there will only be one section on Grover Cleveland, even though he served two seperate terms and is counted as two presidents of the United States. I hope you enjoy reading this book and maybe take away some new facts you did not know.

George Washington

Name: George Washington

Date of Birth: 22nd February 1732

Place of Birth: Westmoreland, Virginia

President Number:1

Preceded by: N/A

Succeeded By: John Adams

Presidential Years: 1789-1797 (two terms)

Political Party: N/A

Date of death: 14th December 1799

Place of Death: Mount Vernon,Virgina

Facts and Myths

Fact 1: George Washington was considered to be the best horseman in the 13 colonies

Fact 2: Washington is the only president who never ran for president instead he was voted in unaminously on both occasions.

Fact 3: Washington refused payment for over 8years as Commander in Chief asking only to be reimbursed for his expenses this request was never fully met.

Fact 4: He desired no pay as President, but Congress allotted an annual budget of $25,000 for the Executive Branch, from which all salaries of staff and Cabinet members, as well as expenses, would be paid. Most years George Washington had to spend some of his own money to make up the difference.

Fact 5: George Washington fired the first shot tthat started the French-Indian war

Fact 6: George Washington came up with the idea of greeting the Presisent as Mr President as he did not like the more formal suggestions put forward to him

Fact 7: It is thanks to George Washington that America has the two-term tradition for each President

Fact 8: George Washington did not wear a wig

Fact 9: Geotge Washington was so strong he could crack a walnut between his thumb and forefinger

Fact 10: Before the war of independence George Washington fought for the British army

Fact 11: George Washington never fathered any children but he adopted his wife Matrtha's two children and loved them like they were his own

Fact 12: At the age of 57 due to his numerous toothaches George Washington had all his teeth taken out and had false teeth made out of gold,lead and ivory also with animal and human teeth mixed in.

Fact 13: George Washington lost most battles he fought in

Fact 14: George Washington grew Hemp as a cash crop Hemp aswell as a drug has many useful properties it is used to make things such as rope and paper

Fact 15: George Washington is the only man to have gone in to battle while holding the presidential office

Myth 1: The most well known myth about George Washington is the Cherry tree myth. The story goes that when George Washington was a young boy he used a hatchet and chopped down his fathers Cherry tree his father confronted him about it George told his father the truth stating "I cannot tell a lie." to which his father supposedly answered "son your honesty is worth more to me than a thousand cherry trees." this event however did not take place.

Myth 2: There is a myth that George Washington did not like his wife Martha and found her ugly and stupid and it is said that Washington was adultorous however this could not be further from the truth George was totaly devoted to Martha and they loved eachother dearly.

Myth 3: There is a myth that George Washington smoked Marijuana which is false he did however grow hemp for the purpose of selling it for rope and paper making

Myth 4: There is a myth that George Washington had a child with one of his slaves this however is not true

Myth 5: It is said that George Washington died of Syphillis this however is false he died possibly due to loss of blood after multiple attempts at blood letting during an illness.

Myth 6: George Washington did not throw a silver dollar over the Potomac River for the simple fact the iver is around one mile wide also silver dollars were not around at the time this was supposed to have occurred this myth could have been mixed up with the story told by George Washington Parke Curtis reported that George Washington once threw a piece of slate "about the size and shape of a silver dollar" across the Rappahannock River which at 250ft wide is still a herculian but achieveable task.

Myth 7: George Washington is buried under the capitol this is not true George Washington as stated in his will is laid to rest at Mount Vernon although a vault was placed in the Capitol with the intention of placing George Washington there.

Myth 8: George Washington was not the first President. Some people claim the first President of the United States was John Hanson this is just false The Role was not created until 1787 long after John Hanson died

John Adams

Name: John Adams

Date of Birth: 30th October 1735

Place of Birth: Braintree, Massachusetts

President Number: 2

Preceded By: George Washington

Succeeded By: Thomas Jefferson

Presidential Years: 1797-1801 (one term)

Political Party: Federalist

Date of Death: 4th July 1826

Place of Death: Quincy, Massachustetts

Facts and Myths

Fact 1: none of John Adams family was present at his inaugeration.

Fact 2: John Adams did not own slaves but he was against aboloshing slavery

Fact 3: Out of the first five presidents John Adams was the only man who was not from Virginia.

Fact 4 John Adams died on the same day as Thomas Jefferson his last words were reportedly about Jefferson "Thomas Jefferson survives" is what he is reported to have said but Thomas had died hours before.

Fact 5: John Adams son became the sixth president

Fact 6: John Adams defended in court two British soldiers who were involved in the Boston Massacre.

Fact 7: If the British won the war of independence they wanted to have John Adams Hanged.

Fact 8: Adams was the first to propose a military academy.

Fact 9: John Adams personal diary was read aloud and laughed at in congress possibly due to the vanity John Adams showed.

Fact 10: John Adams was the first President to live in the White House

Fact 11: John Adams was a hopeless romantic

Fact 12: In 1797 the home of Andrew Brown (who had been an ardent critic of John Adams) home caught fire and John Adams tried his best to save his enemies home he was seen running back and forth with buckets of water.

Fact 13: John Adams created the worlds first band when he created the United States Marine Band.

Fact 14: The final official dinner that John Adams gave as President was for a delegation of Native Americans.

Myth 1: There was a myth that John Adams took his inaugrual speech from an old Irish pub song called Miss O'Sullivans knickers. This however is not true.

Myth 2: "Nabby" Adams John Adams daughter did not die in 1803 as stated in various places but Nabby was diagnosed with her breast cancer in 1810 and her mastectomy took place in 1811

Myth 3: There has been stories that John and Samuel did not get along. John Adams was never at odds or concerned with the tyranity of his Cousin Samuel Adams as Samuel and John shared many political views and Samuel was not a bad guy as has been depicted in the past.

Myth 4: Bunker hill passed by John Adams house infact the militia line was on the opposite side of the Boston Harbor.

Thomas Jefferson

Name: Thomas Jefferson

Date of Birth: 13th April 1743

Place of Birth: Shadwell, Virginia

President Number: 3

Preceded By: John Adams

Succeeded By: James Madison

Presidential Years: 1801-1809 (two terms)

Political Party: Democratic Republican Party

Date of Death: 4th July 1826

Place of Death: Charlottesville, Virginia

Facts and Myths

Fact 1: Thomas Jefferson wrote the Declaration of Independence.

Fact 2: Thomas Jefferson was a huge fan of books and owned thousands of them even selling thousands to the US Library of Congress.

Fact 3: Thomas Jefferson was a keen astronomer

Fact 4: Thomas Jefferson created the University of Virginia.

Fact 5: Thomas Jefferson was twice a govourner of Virginia

Fact 6: Thomas Jefferson is responsible for the Louisianna Purchase

Fact 7: Jefferson designed his own house which he named Monticello.

Fact 8: Thomas Jefferson had pet Mockingbirds.

Fact 9: Thomas Jefferson loved fossils and once tried to erect a skeleton of an animal that had been extinct for 40 million years.

Fact 10: As a child Thomas Jefferson learned to play the violin.

Myth 1: There is a myth Thomas Jefferson was a heavy drinker in reality he drank in moderation and often watered down his wine.

Myth 2: Thomas Jefferson is said to have been more in favour of states rights than a United Nation. this misconception may have come about because of an anonymous article he had wrote called the Kentucky Resolutions but in fact Thomas Jefferson was a true federalist and wanted to keep power balanced between national and state goverments.

Myth 3: Thomas Jefferson is sometimes labeled as an hypocrite due to the fact he stated "All men are created equal." because he not only owned slaves but also did not emancipate them in his will. However he had inherited his slaves and had publicaly stated that slavery was "An abomination to our creator." and constantly looked for ways to abolish slavery.

James Madison

Name: James Madison

Date of Birth: 16th March 1751

Place of Birth: Port Conway, Virginia

President Number: 4

Preceded By: Thomas Jefferson

Succeeded By: James Monroe

Presidential Years: 1809-1817 (two terms)

Political Party: Democratic Republican Party

Date of Death: 28th June 1836

Place of Death: Orange, Virginia

Facts and Myths

Fact 1: James Madison is known as the father of the constitution.

Fact 2: James Madison asked for the declaration of war against the British which started the war of 1812

Fact 3: At 5ft 4inches and only 100lb James Madison is the smallesy ever president.

Fact 4: He was a key author of the Bill of Rights

Fact 5: James Madison was ill a lot

Fact 6: James Madison fought and won an oratory duel with Patrick Henry which was no easy task.

Fact 7: In 1789 James Madison competed and won against James Monroe for a seat in the House of Representatives

Fact 8: James Madison wanted to hire the Portugese Navy.

Fact 9: James Madison had no biological children.

Fact 10: James Madison used many different codes such as cyphers.

Fact 11: Both of James Madisons Vice Presidents died in office.

Fact 12: Madison became the second rector of the University of Virginia

Myth 1: The secretary of beer myth It is rumoured James Madison wanted to appoint a secretary of beer but congress would not accept this is not true at all.

James Monroe

Name: James Monroe

Date of Birth: 28th April 1758

Place of Birth: Monroe Hall, Virginia

President Number: 5

Preceded By: James Madison

Succeeded By: John Quincy Adams

Presidential Years 1817-1825 (two terms)

Political Party: Democratic Republican Party

Date of Death: 4th July 1831

Place of Death: New York City, New York

Facts and Myths

Fact 1: James Monroe served in the revolutionary war under George Washington.

Fact 2: James suffered a shoulder injury during the Battle of Trenton from which he carried shrapnel in his shoulder for the rest of his life.

Fact 3: James actialy moved to Albemarle County, Virginia just to be close to Thomas Jefferson who was his mentor.

Fact 4: James travelled from Paris to Madrid via a Mule in order to purchase Florida.

Fact 5: James's first term in office was named the era of good feelings.

Fact 6: By the time his second Presidential term ended James had served his country for more than 50yrs in various roles holding more elected public offices than any of the previous Presidents

Fact 7: James Monroe had his portrait painted by Samuel Morse who is famous for inventing the Morse Code.

Fact 8: Liberia capital Monrovia was named after James Monroe and is the only foreign capital named after a US President.

Fact 9: James Monroe was considered the last of the founding fathers

Fact 10: James Monroe died on July 4th making that three out of the of the five presidential founding fathers to die on Independence Day, the other two being John Adams and Thomas Jefferson.

Myth 1: George Washington and James Monroe crossed the Delaware together. This never happened except in a painting in reality James Monroe went a seperate way to George.

Myth 2: Thanks to a wax work of James Monroe and George Washington sharing some rum together some people believe the two men were friends. However the reality is the two men hated each other and were passionate about their dislike for one another.

John Quincy Adams

Name: John Quincy Adams

Date of Birth: 11th July 1767

Place of Birth: Braintree, Massachusetts

President Number: 6

Preceded By: James Monroe

Succeeded By: Andrew Jackson

Presidential Years: 1825-1829 (one term)

Political Party: Democratic Party

Date of Death: 23rd February 1848

Place of Death: Washington D.C

Facts and Myths

Fact 1: John Quincy Adams watched the Battle of Bunker Hill from a hill near his home when he was 8yrs old.

Fact 2: John Quincy suffered from depression

Fact 3: John Quincy's brother and son both died from alcoholism.

Fact 4: John Quincy could speak French, Dutch and German he could also speak Italian Latin and classical Greek.

Fact 5: on 21st February 1848 John Quincy suffered a stroke it occurred when the House of Representatives were discussing a subject he strongly opposed when it came to voting he cried "No!!" and collapsed he died two days later

Fact 6: John Quincy Adams believed the world was hollow and approved an expedition to dig through the north pole in hopes of finding the civilisation living underground.

Myth 1: There is a myth that John Quincy Adams milked cows with his toes this story is untrue.

Andrew Jackson

Name: Andrew Jackson

Date of Birth: 15th March 1767

Place of Birth: Waxhaws

President Number: 7

Preceded By: John Quincy Adams

Succeeded By: Martin Van Buren

Presidential Years: 1829-1837 (two terms)

Political Party: Democratic Party

Date of Death: 8th June 1845

Place of Death: Nashville, Tennessee

Facts and Myths

Fact 1: Andrew Jacksons parents were Irish who emigrated from modern day Northern Ireland

Fact 2: Andrew Jackson was born in the Waxhaws region that sits on the border of both North and South Carolina and both claim to be his birth place.

Fact 3: Andrew Jackson appears on the $20 note even though he hated paper money

Fact 4: Andrew Jackson won the popular vote for President three times

Fact 5:Andrew Jackson competed in anywhere up to 100 duels killing at least one man in the process A man named Charles Dickinson called Andrew a "Worthless scoundrel, a paltroon and a coward." So Alan challenged him to a duel in 1806. At the command Charles shot Andrew in the chest barely missing his heart Jackson did not back down however and managed to raise his pistol and shoot Charles dead. Andrew would carry the bullet in his chest for the rest of his life.

Fact 6: Andrew Jackson's nickname was "Old Hickory" as when he was in the army the soldiers said he was as tough as old hickory wood and the name old hickory stuck.

Fact 7: Andrew Jackson was the subject of the first ever attempt to assassinate a president. This occured on the 30th January 1835 as Andrew was leaving a memorial service for a congressman a house painter named Richard Lawrence fired a pistol at Andrew from just a couple of feet away the gun misfired Richard then pulled out a second gun which also misfired Andrew Jackson set about the would be assassain with his an investigation afterwards found the guns to be in perfect working order and the odds of both guns misfiring was estimated at 125,000 to 1 so Andrew was an extemely lucky man.

Fact 8: Andrew Jackson adopted two Native American children

Fact 9: Andrew Jackson was a notorious gambler and his passion in life was horse racing.

Fact 10: Andrew Jackson is the father of the modern day Democratic party

Fact 11: Andrew was a prisoner of the revolutionary war

Fact 12: Andrew Jackson was a self taught frontier lawyer

Fact 13: Andrew Jackson had a giant 1,400lb cheddar cheese wheel in the White House lobby.

Fact 14: Andrew Jackson was the first and currently only President that had managed to completely pay off the national debt.

Fact 15: Andrew Jackson was the first President to ride on a train.

Fact 16: Andrew Jackson's administration was responsible for the forced relocation of nearly 50,000 Native Americans.

Fact 17: Andrew Jackson had a talking pet parrot which he'd named Poll. At the funeral of Andrew Jackson, the parrot proceeded to screech obscenities and curse words to the mourners, it was quickly removed from the room.

Myth 1: Andrew Jackson was half African this was obviously not true as mentioned above Both Andrews parents were Irish

Myth 2: Andrew Jackson wrote a will leaving everything to a flower bed. This is obviously false

Martin Van Buren

Name: Martin Van Buren

Date of Birth: 5th December 1782

Place of Birth: Kinderhook

President Number: 8

Preceded By: Andrew Jackson

Succeeded By: William Henry Harrison

Presidential Years: 1837-1841 (one term)

Political Party: Democratic Party

Date of Death: 24th July 1862

Place of Death: Kinderhook

Facts and Myths

Fact 1: Martin played a huge role in the election of Andrew Jackson and was thus appointed to his staff.

Fact 2: Martin blocked Texas from being in the Union in 1836.

Fact 3: Martin Van Buren stopped a war between Canadian and Maine over the border of the Aroostook river.

Fact 4: Martin Van Buren was the first America-born President meaning he was the first president born after the reveloutionary war.

Fact 5: He was beaten by a long way in his bid to be elected for a second term in 1840 by William Henry Harrison.

Fact 6: The term "ok" as in "are you ok" was made popular by Martin Van Burens nickname which was Old Kinderhook often abbreviated to OK.

Fact 7: Martin's autobiography failed to mention either his presidency or his late wife

Myth 1: Martin Van Buren had his name legally changed from Marten at the age of 17. This is wrong his given name at birth was Martin so he never changed it at all.

William Henry Harrison

Name: William Henry Harrison

Date of Birth: 9th February 1773

Place of Birth: Charles City County, Virginia

President Number: 9

Preceded By: Martin Van Buren

Succeeded By: John Tyler

Presidential Years: 1841-1841

Political Party: Whig Party

Date of Death: 4th April 1841

Place of Death: Washington D.C

Facts and Myths

Fact 1: William became famous for winning the battle of Tippecanoe

Fact 2: William came from and produced a prominant political family.

Fact 3: William Henry Harrison's supporters gave out free Whiskey and Cider to gain support for his election.

Fact 4: William Henry Harrison made the longest inauguration speech to date.

Fact 5: William's tenure as President lasted just 33 days and he became the first President to die in office

Fact 6: The doctor stated Williams cause of death as pneumonia doctors today believe it could have had more to do with the fact at the time Washington had no sewer system and the marsh where all the human excrement and waste ended up was mere blocks from the White House and it's water supply and he may have contracted diseases related to that.

Fact 7: William Henry Harrison dropped out of medical school

Myth 1: William Henry was killed by an opposing congress member. This is false as told above his death was disease related

John Tyler

Name: John Tyler

Date of Birth: 29th March 1790

Place of Birth: Charles City County, Virginia

President Number: 10

Preceded By: William Henry Harrison

Succeeded By: James K. Polk

Presidential Years: 1841-1845 (one term)

Political Party: Whig Party, Democratic Republican Party

Date of Death: 18th January 1862

Place of Death: Richmond, Virginia

Facts and Myths

Fact 1: John Tyler set up the U S Presidential succession format as it is known today

Fact 2: John Tyler was quite unpopular even within his own party

Fact 3: John Tyler annexed Texas

Fact 4: John Tyler died as a traitor to the United States by switching to the Confederate states during the Civil War.

Fact 5: John Tyler studied Economics and Law

Fact 6: John strongly disagreed with the Misouri Compromise

Fact 7: John's entire cabinet resigned

James K. Polk

Name: James K. Polk

Date of Birth: 2nd November 1795

Place of Birth: Pineville, North Carolina

President Number: 11

Preceded By: John Tyler

Succeeded By: Zachary Taylor

Presidential Years: 1845-1849 (one term)

Political Party: Democratic Party

Date of Death: 15th June 1849

Place of Death: Nashville, Tennessee

Facts and Myths

Fact 1: James was 49yrs old when he became President

Fact 2: James is the only President who also held the role as Speaker of the House of Representatives.

Fact 3: James is known for adding Texas and California to the United States.

Fact 4: The National election day was set by law during James's term in office.

Fact 5: James was well known as a workaholic

Fact 6: James Polk's wife Sarah Childress started the tradition of the Annual White House Thanksgiving dinner.

Fact 7: James placed a ban on alcohol and dancing in the White House

Fact 8: James Knox Polk died of cholera

Myth 1: James k. Polk achieved all his goals. This is false although it is true James deserves to be well noted and achieved a lot of what he set out to do he did not achieve everything.

Zachary Taylor

Name: Zachary Taylor

Date of Birth: 24th November 1784

Place of Birth: Barboursville, Virginia

President Number: 12

Preceded By: James K. Polk

Succeeded By: Millard Fillmore

Presidential Years: 1849-1850 (died in office)

Political Party: Whig Party

Date of Death: 9th July 1850

Place of Death: Washington D.C

Facts and Myths

Fact 1: Zachary Taylor is is a distant relative to fellow Presidents Robert E. Lee, James Madison and Franklin D. Roosevelt

Fact 2: Zachary spent 25 years in the army including winning major victories in the Mexican wars

Fact 3: in 1850 Zachary was considered the most popular man in America

Fact 4: the first time Zachary voted was in 1848 at the age of 62 until that point he had not lived in an area that allowed him to vote.

Fact 5: Zachary Taylor was known as "Old Rough and Ready" due to his untidy dress sense.

Fact 6: Zachary Taylor had an elderly Warhorse at the White House he called Whitney

Fact 7: Zachary owned a large amount of slaves despite this he actively tried to ban the expansion of slavery which angered many people.

Myth 1: Zachary Taylor was poisoned to death. This is false experts have asertained that the most likely cause for Zachary's death was gastroenteritis.

Millard Fillmore

Name: Millard Fillmore

Date of Birth: 7th January 1800

Place of Birth: Summerhill, New York

President Number: 13

Preceded By: Zachary Taylor

Succeeded By: Franklin Pierce

Presidential Years: 1850-1853 (one term)

Political Party: Anti-Masonic Party, Whig Party

Date of Death: 8th March 1874

Place of Death: Buffalo, New York

Facts and Myths

Fact 1: Millard came from a really poor family.

Fact 2: Millard got his political start on the Anti-Masonic ticket which as the name suggests was against Freemasons

Fact 3: Millard did not have a Vice-President:

Fact 4: Millard attempted to defuse the tension between the North and the South.

Fact 5: Millard is not a very popular president

Fact 6: Millard Fillmore was the first President to own a cat in the White House

Fact 7: Millard had the first library installed in the White House

Myth 1: Millard prefered dusting to Presidential duties and let his maids run cabinet meetings while he cleaned. This is simply not true I am flabberghasted as to how anybody believed this.

Myth 2: Millard installed the first bath in the White House this is not true this rumour has been associated with Millard and Pierce But Andrew Jackson had a bathing room when he was President and running water in there.

Franklin Pierce

Name: Franklin Pierce

Date of Birth: 23rd November 1804

Place of Birth: Hillsborough, New Hampshire

President Number: 14

Preceded By: Millard Fillmore:

Succeeded By: James Buchanan

Presidential Years: 1853-1857 (one term)

Political Party: Democratic Party

Date of Death: 8th October 1869

Place of Death: Concord, New Hampshire

Facts and Myths

Fact 1: Franklin Pierce fought in the Mexican war

Fact 2: Franklin Pierce was against the abolition of slavery

Fact 3: Franklin Pierce was an alcoholic

Fact 4: Franklin was criticised for the leaked Ostend Manifesto

Fact 5: Franklin completed the Gadsden Purchase.

Fact 6: Franklin retired to take care of his wife Jane who was grieving over the death of their youngest son.

Fact 7: Franklin was opposed to the civil war.

Myth 1: Franklin Pierce won the 1852 election two days after getting parole from prison. This is not true Pierce was not in prison during the campaign ut rather just kept out of the public eye.

James Buchanan

Name: James Buchanan

Date of Birth: 23rd April 1791

Place of Birth: Cove Gap, Pennsylvania

President Number: 15

Preceded By: Franklin Pierce

Succeeded By: Abraham Lincoln

Presidential Years: 1857-1861 (one term)

Political Party: Democratic Party

Date of Death: 1st June 1868

Place of Death: Lancaster, Pennsylvania

Facts and Myths

Fact 1: James Buchanan was a Homosexual and America's first gay President.

Fact 2: James Buchanan was the first President to wear blue jeans in the Oval Office.

Fact 3: As a child James had a pet named Betty Ross it was an African Gray Parrot.

Fact 4: James had no middle finger on his right hand, he lost it in the war of 1812 during the Battle of Raisen River.

Fact 5: James raised pygmy goats on the White House Rose Garden.

Fact 6: James had two different coloured eyes, one green and one brown.

Fact 7: James Buchanan was a direct descendent of both Cleopatra and King James the first of Scotland.

Fact 8: James was supposed to take part in the Lewis and Clark Expedition but had an unfortunate archery accident involving his buttocks.

Fact 9: During his Presidential term seven Southern States seceded from the Union which brought Civil war closer

Myth 1: James Buchanan never left the Oval Office when President. this is a false statement James Buchanan left the Oval Office on many occasions.

Abraham Lincoln

Name: Abraham Lincoln

Date of Birth: 12th February 1809

Place of Birth: Hodgenville, Kentucky

President Number: 16

Preceded By: James Buchanan

Succeeded By: Andrew Johnson

Presidential Years: 1861-1865 (assassinated)

Political Party: National Union Party

Date of Death: 15th April 1865

Place of Death: Washington D.C

Facts and Myths

Fact 1: Abraham Lincoln wanted women to be allowed to vote in 1836

Fact 2: Abraham was a big animal lover and would never hunt or fish

Fact 3: Abraham was a wrestler there is documented proof of him taking part in bouts.

Fact 4 Abraham Lincoln lost failed in his first bid for a Presidential ticket

Fact 5: Abraham hated being called Abe he prefered the name Lincoln

Fact 6: Abraham Lincoln made Thanksgiving a national holiday.

Fact 7: Lincoln's cat ate at the dinner table.

Fact 8: He was the first President to use the telegraph.

Fact 9: Lincolns mother was killed by poison milk

Fact 10: He was the first President with a beard

Fact 11: He was shot on Good Friday.

Fact 12: Lincoln kept important documents inside his hat.

Myth 1: Lincoln was a simple country lawyer. Lincoln's law partner William H. Herndon, looking to boost his own reputation, introduced the canard that Lincoln cared little about his legal practice, did scant research, joked around with juries and judges, and sometimes failed to collect fees. Lincoln himself may have compromised his legal reputation with his often quoted admonition "Discourage litigation."

True, politics became lawyer Lincoln's chief ambition. Still, in the 1850s he ably and profitably represented the Illinois Central Railroad and the Rock Island Bridge Co, the company that built the first railroad bridge over the Mississippi River and earned a solid reputation as one of his home state's top appeals lawyers.

Myth 2: Abraham Lincoln was gay. Not that it really matters but Abraham Lincoln was not gay he was a happily married man and before his marraige he was a regular visitor to brothels.

Myth 3: Abraham Lincoln owned slaves. Neither Abraham or his father owned slaves.

Myth 4: Abraham Lincoln wrote the Gettysburg Address on the back of an envelope on a train ride to the speech. There are five known manuscript copies of the address and it is widely agreed that this rumour is false.

Andrew Johnson

Name: Andrew Johnson

Date of Birth: 29th December 1808

Place of Birth: Raleigh, North Carolina

President Number: 17

Preceded By: Abraham Lincoln

Succeeded By: Ulysses S. Grant

Presidential Years: 1865-1869 (one term)

Political Party: Democratic Party, National Union Party

Date of Death: 31st July 1875

Place of Death: Elizabethton, Tennessee

Facts and Myths

Fact 1: Andrew along with his brother escaped from Indentured Servitude.

Fact 2: He never attended school.

Fact 3: Andrew became Mayor of Greenville Tennessee at the age of 22

Fact 4: Andrew was the only southerner to retain his seat upon the secession of the southern states.

Fact 5: He presided over Seward's Folly which was the aquisition of Alaska from Russia for $7.2m

Fact 6: He was the first President to be impeached.

Fact 7: Andrew Johnson did not agree with the freeing of slaves.

Fact 8: About his death Andrew Johnson quoted "When I die, I desire no better winding sheet that the Stars and Stripes and no softer pillow that the constitution of my country." He was buried with his body wrapped within the U.S. flag and his copy of the Constitution as a pillow.

Ulysses S. Grant

Name: Ulysses S. Grant

Date of Birth: 27th April 1822

Place of Birth: Point Pleasant, Ohio

President Number: 18

Preceded By: Andrew Johnson

Succeeded: Rutherford B. Hayes

Presidential Years: 1869-1877 (two terms)

Political Party: Republican Party, Democratic Party, National Union Party.

Date of Death: 23rd July 1885

Place of Death: Wilton, New York

Facts and Myths

Fact 1: Ulysses real first name was Hiram

Fact 2: He did not like Andrew Johnson

Fact 3: He tried to Annex the Dominican Republican.

Fact 4: He was a talented writer.

Fact 5: The S in his name does not stand for anything.

Fact 6: He won the first major Union victory of the Civil War.

Fact 7: He was a big drinker so much so he was forced to resign from the army through drinking.alcohol.

Fact 8: He hated wearing army uniforms.

Fact 9: He was supposed to be at the theatre as Lincolns guest the night Lincoln was assassinated but instead had to decline to go see his children with his wife. He described Lincoln's death as "Darkest day of my life."

Fact 10: He prevented Robert E. Lee from being charged with treason after the civil war

Facy 11: He had no experience in politics before he became President.

Fact 12: He was responsible for dismantling the KKK after their uprise in the 1860s this happened in 1871 and they did not resurdace til around 1910

Fact 13: His memoirs were published by Mark Twain.

Myth 1: Ulysses S. Grant was responsible for stopping the prisoner exchanges during the civil war. This is not true, though he is quoted as saying it was a bad thing because every prisoner given back was another man to take up arms against them, at the time the prisoner exchanges were stopped, he was just a commander in the west and so would of had little to no influence in those matters with the prisoners, it was not til the following year he was promoted to Commander of all Union Armies.

Rutherford B. Hayes

Name: Rutherford B. Hayes

Date of Birth: 4th October 1822

Place of Birth: Delaware, Ohio

President Number: 19

Preceded By: Ulysses S. Grant

Succeeded By: James A. Garfield

Presidential Years: 1877-1881 (one term)

Political Party: Whig Party, Republican Party

Date of Death: 17th January 1893

Place of Death: Fremont, Ohio

Facts and Myths

Fact 1: He was the first president to use a telephone.

Fact 2: He suffered multiple wounds in the Civil War

Fact 3: Hayes and his wife conducted the first Easter Egg Roll in the White House.

Fact 4: He signed a legislation to allow women in the court room.

Fact 5: The Election of 1876 was highly controversial. The electoral votes from four states were contested and a Congressional commission had to be set up to resolve the dispute. The bi-partisan commission granted the disputed electoral votes to Hayes, giving him the presidency by one vote.

Fact 6: Hayes was sworn in in secrecy due to the controversy of his election

Fact 7: He refused to run for a second term

Myth 1: Hayes did not do enough for reform and was destroying spoilsmen operations. This is not true Rutherford introduce all the reform that he could without destroying the Republican party organizations.

James A. Garfield

Name: James A. Garfield

Date of Birth: 19th November 1831

Place of Birth: Moreland Hills,Ohio

President Number: 20

Preceded By: Rutherford B. Hayes

Succeeded By: Chester A. Arthur

Presidential Term: 1881-1881 (assassinated)

Political Party: Republican Party

Date of Death: 19th September 1881

Place of Death: Elberon, New Jersey

Facts and Myths

Fact 1: He was the first left handed President

Fact 2: He was a preacher

Fact 3: He campaigned in multiple languages including German

Fact 4: He was assassinated on 19th September 1881 by a republican named Charles J. Guiteau

Fact 5: He was a Major General during the Civil War.

Fact 6: He was part of the committee that gave the Presidency to Rutherford B. Hayes

Myth 1: A left wing radical Democrat shot James Garfield. This is false Garfield's assassain was a member of his own Republican Party and believed God told him to do it.

Chester A. Arthur

Name: Chester A. Arthur

Date of Birth: 5th October 1829

Place of Birth: Fairfield, Vermont

President Number: 21

Preceded By: James A. Garfield

Succeeded By: Grover Cleveland

Presidential Years: 1881-1885 (one term)

Political Party: Republican Party

Date of Death 18th November 1886

Place of Death: Manhattan, New York

Facts and Myths

Fact 1: He sometimes lied about his age

Fact 2: He was named after the doctor who delivered him

Fact 3: He helped throw his colleges school bell in the Erie Canal as a prank.

Fact 4: In college he fought in brawls against James K. Polk supporters

Fact 5: He stayed awake til at least 2am every night

Fact 6: People suspected he had something to do with the shooting of James Garfield

Fact 7: He had no Vice President

Fact 8: He did not run for a second term election due to him having kidney problems

Myth 1: Chester A. Arthur was born in Canada. This is not true Chester's parents spent time in both Ireland and Canada before he was born. But Chester was born in Fairfield, Vermont, USA.

Grover Cleveland

Name: Grover Cleveland

Date of Birth: 18th March 1837

Place of Birth: Caldwell, New Jersey

President Number: 22 and 24

Preceded By: Chester A. Arthur/ Benjamin Harrison

Succeeded By: Benjamin Harrison/ William McKinley

Presidential Years 1885-1889 (one term)/ 1893-1897 (one term)

Political Party: Democratic Party

Date of Death: 24th June 1908

Place of Death: Priceton, New Jersey

Facts and Myths

Fact 1: He is the only man to serve two non-consecutive terms as President

Fact 2: His real first name was Stephen

Fact 3: Before pursuing a career in law Grover was a teacher at New York Institute for the Blind

Fact 4: Grover was honest when asked if he had fathered an illegitimate child he stated it is possible the child was his which blunted any impact the scandal may have otherwise had

Fact 5: Grover Cleveland was drafted during the Civil War, however, he paid the sum of $150 for a Polish immigrant George Brinske to serve in his place. This was a lawful option, but later political rivals raised questions about his lack of duty.

Fact 6: His wedding ceremony was held at the White House.

Fact 7: Due to his size he was nnamed "Big Steve" and "Uncle Jumbo"

Fact 8: He was the first President to be filmed it occurred in 1895 as he was signing a new bill into law.

Fact 9: The Statue of Liberty was dedicated by Grover Cleveland on October 28, 1886. Originally the statue was known as "Liberty Enlightening the World," it was a gift from the people of France and stands 151 ft (46m) high.

Fact 10: Grover Cleveland was quoted as saying "Whatever you do tell the truth."

Benjamin Harrison

Name: Benjamin Harrison

Date of Birth: 20th August 1833

Place of Birth: North Bend, Ohio

President Number: 23

Preceded By: Grover Cleveland

Succeeded By: Grover Cleveland

Presidential Years: 1889-1893 (one term)

Political Party: Republican Party

Date of Death: 13th March 1901

Place of Death: Indianapolis, Indiana

Facts an Myths

Fact 1: He was the Grandson of William Henry Harrison.

Fact 2: He was the first President to use electricity in the White House.

Fact 3: He was known as "The Human Iceberg" due to the manner in which he dealt with people.

Fact 4: He was the first President who's congress had an annual spending of over $1bn

Fact 5: Benjamin Harrison endorsed the passing of the 'Sherman Silver Purchase Act', this enabled the government to purchase more silver than had previously been agreed.

Fact 6: As president Benjamin Harrison appointed the first African-American a high ranking role in government. Frederick Douglass was a former slave and became minister to Haiti in 1889.

Fact 7: The voice of Benjamin Harrison was recorded on wax phonograph cylinder in 1889, the 36 second recording is the first voice of a president known to be preserved.

William McKinley

Name: William McKinley

Date of Birth: 29th January 1843

Place of Birth: Niles, Ohio

President Number: 25

Preceded By: Grover Cleveland

Succeeded By: Theodore Roosevelt

Presidential Years: 1897-1901(two terms/assassinated
months into his second term)

Political Party: Republican Party

Date of Death: 14th September 1901

Place of Death: Buffalo, New York

Facts and Myths

Fact 1: He was the first President to eide in an automobile

Fact 2: he told his men not to let the crowd hurt the man who shot him

Fact 3: He appeared on the $500 bill

Fact 4: His inauguration was the first to be filmed

Fact 5: He loved red Carnations and believed they brought him luck

Fact 6: He played a big part in the Annexation of Hawaii

Fact 7: He had a Parrot name Washington Post that could whistle the tune to Yankee Doodle

Theodore Roosevelt

Name: Theodore Roosevelt

Date of Birth: 27th October 1858

Place of Birth: Manhattan, New York

President Number: 26

Preceded By: William McKinley

Succeeded By: William H. Taft

Presidential Years: 1901-1909 (two terms)

Political Party: Republican Party, Progressive Party

Date of Death: 6th January 1919

Place of Death: Cove Neck, New York

Facts and Myths

Fact 1: He participated in a boxing match hat left him blind in one eye.

Fact 2: His mum and his wife both died on Valentines day

Fact 3: He was a police man in New York

Fact 4: Heowent skinny dipping in the Potomac River

Fact 5: He won the Nobel Peace Prize

Fact 6: He was the first President to leave the Country while in office.

Fact 7: He was a prolific author

Fact 8: The Republican leaders did not really want Theodore as President nobody thought he would take over from McKinley in 1901 as he was originally going to run in 1904

Fact 9: He was the father of the modern U S Navy.

Fact 10: While on a hunting trip guides in Mississippi had arranged for Roosevelt to shoot an old bear they had tied to a tree. Roosevelt refused to do so, on sporting grounds. Instead, he had someone else shoot the bear. The first part of the incident became a newspaper cartoon, which then inspired a shopkeeper to sell stuffed bears, with Roosevelt's permission.

Fact 11: He was shot while giving a speech and still continued to give the 90 minute speech with a bullet in his chest, simply stating " I was going to make a very long speech, and there is a bullet...The bullet is in me now so that i cannot make a very long speech but i will try my best."

Fact 12: He loved Celtic Mythology

Myth 1: Theodore Roosevelt rode a Moose. This is not true it came from a picture that was doctored in what i suppose was an early form of photoschop that cut to pictures together that led to this myth being believed.

William Howard Taft

Name: William Howard Taft

Date: of Birth: 15th September 1857

Place: Cincinnati,Ohio

President Number: 27

Preceded By: Theodore Roosevelt

Succeeded By: Woodrow Wilson

Presidential Years: 1909-1913 (one term)

Political Party: Republican Party

Date of Death: 8th March 1930

Place of Death: Washington D.C

Facts and Myths

Fact 1: He was the last President to have facial hair while in office.

Fact 2: He valued his position at the Supreme Court more than being President.

Fact 3: He debuted the Presidential first pitch when Hall of Famer Walter Johnson managed to snag a low flying ball that William had threw from the stands in 1910

Fact 4: As Chief Justice he swore in two other Presidents Calvin Coolidge and Herbert Hoover.

Fact 5: He had worked as a part-time reporter.

Fact 6: He lost 70 pounds in weight after leaving the White House

Fact 7: He often fell asleep at public funtions leading his wife to nickname him "Sleeping Beauty"

Fact 8: He successfully lobbied for the modern Supreme Court building.

Fact 9: Taft once got into a hotel bath tub and spilled a lot of dirty water out it seeped through the floor and on to peoples heads the level below him.

Fact 10: He was a wrestler at Yale

Fact 11: Taft was tone deaf.

Fact 11: Taft was the first President to own a car and he converted the stables into a garage.

Myth 1: William Howard Taft got stuck in the bath tub. While it is true he was not called Big Bill for nothing this story is a fabrication that somehow got taken as fact.

<u>Woodrow Wilson</u>

Name: Woodrow Wilson

Date of Birth: 28th December 1856

Place of Birth: Stauntan, Virginia

President Number 28

Preceded By: William Howard Taft

Succeeded By: Warren G. Harding

Presidential Years: 1913-1921 (two terms)

Political Party: Democratic Party

Date of Death: 3rd February 1924

Place of Death: Washigton D.C

Facts and Myths

Fact 1: He was a professional Historian and a Political Scientest

Fact 2: Wilson attended Princeton graduating 38th in a class of 167

Fact 3 He fought against fierce opposition in order to hire Louis Brandeis as a Supreme Court Justice. Wilson won and thus hired the first Jewish man to the Supreme Court

Fact 4: He attempted to keep the United States out of WW1 he failed to do so however.

Fact 5: After WW1 he founded the League of Nations

Fact 6: He supported Immigration rights and vetoed anti-immigration legislations

Fact 7: He believed in segregation ans allowed it in his goverment departments to an extent that had not been seen before. in his book "History of the American people" there is a quote that goes as follows " The white men were roused by a mere instinct of self-presevation....until at last there had sprung into existence a great Klu Klux Klan a veritable empire of the South to protect the Southern country."

Fact 8: He took military action against Pancho Villa

Fact 9: He created his 14 points for world peace

Myth 1: Woodrow Wilson had an affair with Florence La Badie. This did not happen

Myth 2: Woodrow Wilson killed Florence La Badie to keep her quiet. Again giving the affair did not happen their was no need for him to kill her this again is false.

Warren G. Harding

Name: Warren G Harding

Date of Birth: 2nd November 1865

Place of Birth: Blooming Grove, Ohio

President Number: 29

Preceded By: Woodrow Wilson

Succeeded By: Calvin Coolidge

Presidential Years: 1921-1923 (one term died in office)

Political Party: Republican Party

Date of Death: 2nd August 1923

Place of Death: San Francisco, California

Facts and Myths

Fact 1: He had many affairs and no stranger to adultery

Fact 2: He died as his wife was reading him a favourible review

Fact 3: He owned the Marion Daily Star newspaper

Fact 4: He reveloutionized the campaigning for the first time using newsreels and photo oppurtunities that became the norm and campaign results were broadcast on radio

Fact 5: His Presidency was full of scandal with many different events including bribery from oil companies

Myth 1: Warren G. Harding was descended from African-Americans. This is not true it was part of a smear campaign.

Calvin Coolidge

Name: Calvin Coolidge

Date of Birth: 4th July 1872

Place of Birth: Plymouth Notch, Vermont

President Number: 30

Preceded By: Warren G. Harding

Succeded By: Herbert Hoover

Presidential Years: 1923-1929 (two terms/one term plus end of Warren G. Hardings term)

Political Party: Republican Party

Date of Death: 5th January 1933

Place of Death: Northampton, Massachusetts

Facts and Myths

Fact 1: He was a supporter of lower taxes and smaller govoerments.

Fact 2: He was good with the media

Fact 3: He fought corruption at the highest levels

Fact 4: He regulated radio broadcast frequencies

Fact 5: Even though he was a good public speaker he earned the name "Silent Cal" for his withdrawn personality at social occasions.

Fact 6: He opted not to run for President in 1928 as it would have meant 10yrs as President.

Herbert Hoover

Name: Herbert Hoover

Date of Birth: 10th August 1874

Place of Birth: West Branch, Iowa

President Number: 31

Preceded By: Calvin Coolidge

Succeeded By: Franklin D. Roosevelt

Presidential Years: 1929-1939 (one term)

Political Party: Republican Party

Date of Death: 20th October 1964

Place of Death: New York City, New York

Facts and Myths

Fact 1: He became an orphan at the age of 9

Fact 2: He was a self made multi-millionaire

Fact 3: He helped save millions of people from starvation after two world wars.

Fact 4: After his humanitarian work both Republicans and Democrats Wanted Herbert to become President

Fact 5: He starrec in the first television broadcast in American history

Fact 6: There is a sport named after him which was developed by his physician as a way of keeping him fit

Fact 7: He was not invited to the dedication of the Hoover Dam

Fact 8: He could speak Chinese and he and his wife did so whenever they wanted a private conversation

Fact 9: Herbert Hoover was caught up in the Boxer Rebellion whilst working in China

Myth 1: Herbert Hoover was a do nothing President before and during the Great Depression. Not so Herbert gave many warnings about the stock market in hopes of preventing it and worked tirelessly to combat it during his term the image of him being a do nothing President has been widely accepted to be propeganda.

Franklin D. Roosevelt

Name: Franklin D. Roosevelt

Date of Birth: 3Oth January 1882

Place of Birth: Hyde Park, New York

President Number: 32

Preceded By: Herbert Hoover

Succeded By: Harry S. Truman

Presidential Years: 1933-1945 (three terms)

Political Party: Democratic Party

Date of Death: 12th April 1945

Place of Death: Warm Springs, Georgia

Facts and Myths

Fact 1: The D in his name stands for Delano

Fact 2: He was a Philanthropist he began his stamp collection at the age of 8

Fact 3: He enjoyed works by Rudyard Kippling, Charles Dokens and Mark Twain

Fact 4: He was once Manager of the Baseball team at Harvard College

Fact 5: He suffered from Polio Which paralized him from the waist down.

Fact 6: He had a gentlemans agreement with the press that they would not publish any photographs of him in his wheelchair.

Fact 7: He considered himself a tree farmer and his favourite tree was The Tulip Poplar.

Fact 8: His favourite song was "Home on the range"

Fact 9: He was a member of a Masonic lodge

Fact 10: He won his elections with landslide victories

Fact 11: No President will ever serve longer after he served 12yrs it was considered that it could be bad for democracy for that to happen again which resulted in the 22nd amendment that no President shall be elected more than twice.

Fact 12: He tried to increase the size of the Supreme Court

Fact 13: He sanctioned the imprisonment of Japanese-Americans.

Fact 14: He was the first President to fly in a plane

.

Harry S. Truman

Name: Harry S Truman

Date of Birth: 8th May 1884

Place of Birth: Lamar, Missouri

President Number: 33

Preceded By: Franklin D. Roosevelt

Succeeded By: Dwight D. Eisenhower

Presidential Years: 1945-1953 (two terms)

Political Party: Democratic Party

Date of Death: 26th December 1972

Place of Death: Kansas City, Missouri

Facts and Myths

Fact 1: The S in Harry S. Truman did not stand for anything his middle name actually was S

Fact 2: He was an artilary commander during WW1

Fact 3: Franklin D. Roosevelt kept Harry in the dark on matters of war.

Fact 4: Harry was not first choice candidate for Senate

Fact 5: The press were so sure Truman was going to lose that they ran a front page with the headline Dewey defeats Truman leading to the infamous picture of Truman holding it up for a photo opportunity.

Fact 7: He had a plaque on his desk that said " The Buck Stops Here"

Fact 8: He made the decision to drop the atomic bomb on Japan in 1945 he felt it neccessary to end the war as quickly as possible.

Fact 9: In 1919 Harry married the love of his life Elizabeth Virginia Wallace who he affectionately named Bess. The pair met in sunday school when he was 6yrs old.

Fact 10: He survived an assassination attempt.

Fact 11: he is responsible for the quote " Ifyou can't stand the heat, get out of the kitchen." and also "If you want a friend in Washington, get a dog."

Dwight D. Eisenhower

Name: Dwight D. Eisenhower

Date of Birth: 14th October 1890

Place of Birth: Denison, Texas

President Number: 34

Preceded By: Harry S. Truman

Succeeded By: John F. Kennedy

Presidential Years: 1953-1961 (two terms)

Political Party: Republican Party

Date of Death: 28th March 1989

Place of Death: Washington D.C

Facts and Myths

Fact 1: He launched the Space Race

Fact 2: He was a 5-star general

Fact 3: His real name was David Dwight Eisenhower

Fact 4: He named Cap David after his Grandson

Fact 5: His first son died of Scarlet Fever

Fact 6: He was President of Columbia University

Fact 7: He loved to paint

Fact 8: He was the first President to ride in a helicopter.

Myth 1: Eisenhower forced German civilians from Weinar to march 5 miles to see the dead bodies at the Buchenwald prison camp. According to General George S. Patton who was there that day it was General Walton Walker who ordered this and Eisenhower never went to the prison camp he visited a camp at Ohrdruf.

Myth 2: Eisenhower was incencitive to Civil Rights and even considered a racist. This story is not true and started with a man named Stephen Ambrose.

John F. Kennedy

Name: John F. Kennedy

Date of Birth: 29th May 1917

Place of Birth: Brookline, Massachusetts

President Number: 35

Preceded By: Dwight D. Eisenhower

Succeeded By: Lyndon B. Johnson

Presidential Years: 1961-1963 (one term/assassinated)

Political Party: Democratic Party

Date of Death: 22nd November 1963

Place of Death: Dallas, Texas

Facts and Myths

Fact 1: He had four children

Fact 2: He was the first Catholic President

Fact 3: He was mediically disqualified from army service

Fact 4: He won a Pultzer Prize

Fact 5: He donated his entire legislative salary to various charities

Fact 6: He installed a secret taping system in the White House

Fact 7: In 1963 he proposed a joint space misssion with the Soviet Union

Fact 8: He has an airport named after him

Fact 9: He doodled a lot

Myth 1: The JFK-Nixon TV debates propelled Kennedy to victory. The four televised debates were the great innovation of the 1960 presidential race, and Sen. Kennedy's impressive appearance and performance at the first one on 26th September gave his campaign a jolt of energy. But Vice President Richard Nixon stepped up his game in the remaining three, especially the final one on foreign policy, a strength of his. While polls were much less frequent in 1960 than today, Gallup has enough data to show that the JFK-Nixon matchup was close throughout. From mid-August onward, the candidates were essentially tied, before and after the debates. Any boost Kennedy got from the first debate disappeared before Election Day. President Dwight Eisenhower, still quite popular, campaigned for Nixon in the race's final days, contributing to the photo finish in the popular vote: 49.72 percent for Kennedy, 49.55 percent for Nixon; out of about 69 million votes cast, JFK won by about 119,000. Sure, the debates were memorable and precedent-setting, but they were by no means decisive.

Myth 2: JFK was a liberal president. This view is widely held today, both because Kennedy is now associated with the civil rights movement and because his legacy is lumped together with those of his late brothers, the much more liberal Bobby and Ted. The brothers followed Jack's moderate lead while he lived, but both became more openly progressive later on. In reality, JFK was a cautious, conservative chief executive, mindful of his 1964 reelection bid after the squeaker of 1960. He was fiscally conservative, careful about spending and deficits, and sponsored an across-the-board tax cut that became President Ronald Reagan's model for his 1981 tax cut. While he was more conciliatory after the Cuban missile crisis, JFK's early Cold War rhetoric was so hawkish that Reagan and other Republicans later quoted him at every opportunity to buttress their fight against communism. And Kennedy was so hesitant and timid about civil rights that he frustrated the movement's leaders at virtually every turn until finally articulating a vision for equal rights in June 1963.

Myth 3: Kennedy was determined to land Americans on the moon. That's how we recall it, because of JFK's blunt declarations to Congress and the public beginning in May 1961, yet Kennedy actively considered alternatives. He actually wanted to send astronauts to Mars but had to be talked out of it because it was so impractical. Once he lowered his sights to our lunar satellite, Kennedy continued to have doubts because of the cost. "Why should we spend that kind of dough to put a man on the moon?" he asked NASA Administrator James Webb in September 1963. Kennedy as mentioned in the fact section even approached Soviet premier Nikita Khrushchev about ending the superpower space race and establishing a Soviet-American partnership for a moon landing. Khrushchev responded favorably, and JFK mentioned it in his fall 1963 speech to the United Nations. His order to NASA to "make it happen" fell by the wayside in the next administration.

Lyndon B. Johnson

Name: Lyndon B. Johnson

Date of Birth: 27th August 1908

Place of Birth: Stonewall, Texas

President Number: 36

Preceded By: John F. Kennedy

Succeeded By: Richard Nixon

Presidential Years: 1963-1969 (two terms/ one elected term)

Political Party: Democratic Party

Date of Death: 22nd January 1973

Place of Death: Stonewall, Texas

Facts and Myths

Fact 1: He was a teacher before he entered politics.

Fact 2: Johnson was nearly killed in World War II. Johnson entered the Naval Reserves while still a Congressman, and on his only bombing run in the South Pacific, he boarded a plane called the Wabash Cannonball for his mission. A last-second trip off the plane to use a bathroom saved Johnson's life. On his return from the facilities, Johnson boarded another plane that survived the mission. The Wabash Cannonball crashed, with a total loss of life.

 Fact 3: The Johnson presidency was incredibly active. In addition to pursuing the Vietnam War, President Johnson pressed on with an expansive slate of programs labeled as the Great Society that included three landmark Civil Rights bills and Medicare. But Vietnam's impact damaged Johnson's political base severely and he declined to run in the 1968 presidential election.

Fact 4: He loved to give gifts he had electric toothbrushes with the Presidents swal commissioned in order to give to friends.

Fact 5: Johnson istaled a fountain in the Oval office that dispensed Fresca.

Fact 6: the wedding ring he gave his wife cost $2.50 from Sears

Richard Nixon

Name: Richard Nixon

Date of Birth: 9th January 1913

Place of Birth: Yorba Linda, California

President Number: 37

Preceded By: Lyndon B. Johnson

Succeeded By: Gerald Ford

Presidential Years: 1969-1974 (two terms/resigned during second term)

Political Party: Republican Party

Date of Death: 22nd April 1994

Place of Death: Manhatton, New York

Facts and Myths

Fact 1: Richards middle name of Milhous was his mother's maiden name

Fact 2: He met his wife Thelma "Pat" while both met while they were auditioning for a theatre production of The Dark Tower

Fact 3: He was a Quaker, who attended four Quaker meetings on sundays as a boy.

Fact 4: He could play five musical instruments they were the Piano, Clarinet, Saxophone, Accordian and Violin.

Fact 5: He loved ten pin bowling and had a one lane alley built in the basement beneath the North Portico entrance to the White House.

Fact 6: He loved Football and was friends with George Allen who was coach of NFL side Washington Redskins.

Fact 7: He had a failed Orange Juice business.

Fact 8: He served in the U.S Navy and served in the South Pacific During WW2

Fact 9: He visited Moscow in 1959 ro open the U.S trade fair.

Fact 10: He initiated the efforts to achieve peace with honour and end the Vietnam war

Fact 11: He was the first President to make an official State visit to the Soviet Union.

Fact 12: Supported Isreal with aid during the Yom Kippur wars which PM Golda meir said saved her country.

Fact 13: Resigned from the role of President in 1974 in the aftermath of Watergate

Fact 14: Wrote ten best sellers.

Myth 1: Nixon ran his election campaign claiming a secret plan to end the Vietnam war. This is not true he never made such claims.

Myth 2: Nixon did not challenge the 1960 election result. While it is true he did not publicaly challenge it behind closed doors he and his allies pursued the matter vigorously.

Myth 3: Nixon and Kennedy were like chalk and cheese and could not agree on anything: Not true although during their campaign they did play up to the rivalry they were on the same side and shared many of the same polocies and thoughts.

Gerald Ford

Name: Gerald Ford

Date of Birth: 14th July 1914

Place of Birth: Omaha, Nebraska

President Number: 38

Preceded By: Richard Nixon

Succeded By: Jimmy Carter

Presidential Years: 1974-1977 (one term)

Political Party: Republican Party

Date of Death: 26th December 2006

Place of Death: Ranch Mirage, California

Facts and Myths

Fact 1: His birth name was Leslie Lynch King Jr

Fact 2: He is the only President to achieve the rank of Eagle Scout

Fact 3: He was a Centre on the football team that won the 1930 State Championship.

Fact 4: Both The Detroit Lions and The Green Bay Packers made offers for him to join them in the NFL

Fact 5: Following the attack at Pearl Harbor Ford joined the Naval Reserves and began his service on the USS Monterey.

Fact 6: In December 1944 he came within inches of being swept overboard.

Fact 7: In 1973 the U.S Senate voted 92-3 in favour of promoting Ford to Vice-President

Fact 8: He was thee first President to appear on Saturday Night Live.

Fact 9: Gerald and Betty Ford received the Congressional Gold Medal on 27th August 1998 for "dedicated public service and outstanding humanitarian contributions to the people of the Untied States." Theirs is the first Gold Medal awarded by Congress jointly to a former President and First Lady.

Fact 10: He won the Presidential Medal Of Freedom the USA's highest civilian decoration.

Fact 11: He recieved the John F. Kennedy Profile in Courage award for choosing to pardon Richard Nixon

Myth 1: Gerald Ford tampered with documents concerning JFK's assassination moving the wound from being upper back to neck in order to sipport the single bullet theory. Not true the reason Gerald did this is because the document stated the wound was in the upper back slightly above the shoulders. Slightly above the shoulders is the neck he was just correcting a possible mistake.

Jimmy Carter

Name: Jimmy Carter

Date of Birth: 1st October 1924

Place of Birth: Plains, Georgia

President Number: 39

Preceded By: Gerald Ford

Succeeded By: Ronald Reagan

Presidential Years: 1977-1981

Political Party: Democratic Party

Date of Death: N/A

Place of Death: N/A

Facts and Myths

Fact 1: He was the first President to be born in a hospital.

Fact 2: He created the Department of Energy:

Fact 3: He liked Bluegras, Country and folk music.

Fact 4: He played a lot of tennis

Fact 5: He collected bottles and arrowheads.

Fact 6: He successfully panned for gold in North Georgia.

Fact 7: He stole money from a church collection plate when he was a young child.

Fact 8: After his sister threw a wrench at him he shot her in the backside with a BB gun

Fact 9: He was able to speed read at a pace of around 2,000 words a minute.

Fact 10: He initiated the Camp David Peace Agreement, This was a contract of resolution between Isreal and Egypt

Fact 11: It was thanks to his daughters school project that the White House trees are marked with the common name Latin name who planted and where they originate.

Fact 12: He was awarded the Nobel Peace Prize in 2002

Myth 1: Carter ruined the economy and needed Reagan to save it. Carter cannot be blamed for the double-digit inflation that peaked on his watch, because inflation started growing in 1965 and snowballed for the next 15 years. To battle inflation, Carter appointed Paul Volcker as Chairman of the Federal Reserve Board, who defeated it by putting the nation through an intentional recession. Once the threat of inflation abated in late 1982, Volcker cut interest rates and flooded the economy with money, fueling an expansion that lasted seven years. Neither Carter nor Reagan had much to do with the economic events that occurred during their terms.

Ronald Reagan

Name: Ronald Reagan

Date of Birth: 6th February 1911

Place of Birth: Tampico, Illinois

Presidemt Number:40

Preceded By: Jimmy Carter

Succeeded By: George H.W.Bush

Presidential Years: 1981-1989 (two terms)

Political Party: Republican Party

Date of Death: 5th June 2004

Place of Birth: Bel-Air, Los Angeles, California

Facts and Myths

Fact 1: He loved to eat jelly beans.

Fact 2: He made his last movie appearence in The Killers in 1964 and was his only role as a villain

Fact 3: After he was injured in a filming accident when a gun was fired next to his hear he had lost partial hearing in one ear.

Fact 4: At a young age he was a Democrat supporter.

Fact 5: He is the only President at the time of writing to have gotten a divorce.

Fact 6: He was a lifeguard at a park in Illinois.

Fact 7: In his bid for re-election against Walter Mondale in 1984 he secured 525 electoral votes which is more than any President in history He achieved 58.8% and won 49 states.

Fact 8: He made the military GPS system available for civilian use.

Fact 9: He survived an assassination attempt when a bullet pierced his lung causing internal bleeding he commented " I forgot to duck."

Fact 10: He presided over the Iran-Contra scandal were firearms were sold to Niciragua

Myth 1: He was the original choice for the lead in Casablanca. This is not true it was always meant to Humphrey Bogart.

George H.W.Bush

Name: George H.W.Bush

Date of Birth: 12th June 1924

Place of Birth: Milton, Massachusetts

President Number: 41

Preceded By: Ronald Reagan

Succeeded By: Bill Clinton

Presidential Years: 1989-1993 (one term)

Political Party: Republican Party

Date of Death: N/A

Place of Death: N/A

Facts and Myths

Fact 1: In 1943 He was the youngest pilot in the Navy and flre 58 missions during WW2

Fact 2: He was captain of Yale University Baseball team

Fact 3: He shaved his head in 2013 in honor of the son of a secret service agent who suffered from Leukemia

Fact 4: He started his own oil company and did well

Fact 5: The H.W stands for Herbert Walker.

Fact 6: Bush gained a wealth of experience in a few years. In the 1970s, Bush was the ambassador to the United Nations, the chairman of the Republican National Committee, the U.S. envoy to China, and the director of the CIA all before 1977

Fact 7: In 1989, Noriega the leader of Panama declared a state of war with the US. Code-named Operation Just Cause, George H.W. Bush sent troops into Panama to successfully regain control. It was a brief war last from 20th December 1989 until 31st January 1990

Fact 8: In the 1990, the US was involved in its second military action with George H. Bush as president. The Persian Gulf War freed Kuwait from Iraqi invaders led by Saddam Hussein. Iraq retreated and the actions of George H. Bush massively increased his popularity

Fact 9: In May 1989, George Bush signed a bill which established a Federal Holiday in the memory of Martin Luther King Jr.

Bill Clinton

Name: Bill Clinton

Date of Birth: 19th August 1946

Place of Birth: Hope, Arkansas

President Number 42

Preceded By: George H.W.Bush

Succeeded By: George W.Bush

Presidential Years: 1993-2001 (two terms)

Political Party: Democratic Party

Date of Death: N/A

Place of Death: N/A

Facts and Myths

Fact 1: His birth name was William Jefferson Blyth

Fact 2: He was the first Democrat since Franklin D. Roosevelt to be elected for two terms

Fact 3: He is left handed

Fact 4: He is the only President who was a Rhodes Scholar.

Fact 5: He is an excellent Saxophone player.

Fact 6: Dr. Martin Luther King Jr.'s "I Have a Dream" speech so impressed a teenaged Clinton that he memorized the entire speech right after it was given.

Fact 7: He was raised by his Grandparents

Fact 8: He has won two Grammy awards

Fact 9: He is the second President to be impeached. America was shocked to hear claims that President Bill

Clinton was involved in a relationship with 22-year-old Monica Lewinsky, which he denied both publicly and under oath. He later accepted that he had had "inappropriate intimate contact" with Lewinsky, his previous denials consequently led to his impeachment of office in 1998

Fact 10: Early into his presidency Bill Clinton endorsed the Family and Medical Leave Act, this paper would allow staff to take unpaid time off work due to pregnancy or critical medical conditions.

Fact 11: In 1994 investigations began into the Whitewater Scandal. The controversy involved real estate investments and the acquisition of land for the Whitewater Development Corporation, which was associated with the Bill and Hillary Clinton and their colleagues Jim and Susan McDougal, the deal failed and accusations of obstruction of justice and fraud followed. The Clinton's were found to be not guilty, but the publicity blemished their popularity in his first term of presidency

Fact 12: On 26th February 1993 a bomb exploded at the World Trade Center in New York City. The terrorist attack killed six people and injured over a thousand. The following day Bill Clinton publically addressed America with an announcement.

Fact 13: On 19th April 1995 a terrorist bombing occurred but this time the terrorist was American. Timothy James "Tim" McVeigh carried out the attack; know as Oklahoma City Bombing because of his hatred of Federal government. It was the most damaging act of U.S. terrorism at the time causing 168 deaths, 19 of which were young children, and injuring another 680. Over 320 buildings were also destroyed or declared inhabitable. About the attack President Bill Clinton said "The bombing in Oklahoma City was an attack on innocent children and defenceless citizens. It was an act of cowardice, and it was evil". Timothy James "Tim" McVeigh was convicted and sentenced to death

Fact 14: He is the first President who's wife (Hilary) has also run for public office.

Fact 14: He has undergone Heart surgery

Fact 15: When asked what he thought about being a president Bill Clinton said "Being president is like running a cemetery: you've got a lot of people under you and nobody's listening"

George W.Bush

Name: George W.Bush

Date of Birth 6th July 1946

Place of Birth: New Haven, Conneticut

President Number: 43

Preceded By: Bill Clinton

Succeded By: Barack Obama

Presidential Years: 2001-2009 (two terms)

Political Party: Republican Party

Date of Death N/A

Place of Death: N/A

Facts and Myths

Fact 1: He has had both the highest and lowest approval ratings in history.

Fact 2: He is the only President to earn an MBA

Fact 3: The 2002 State of the Union address was the first to broadcast live on the Internet.

Fact 4: He ran the 1993 Houston Marathon in a time of 3hrs 44mins and was the first President to have finished a Marathon at some point in their life

Fact 5: He was a cheerleader at his alma mater.

Fact 6: He was arrested during his college days for stealing a christmas wreath from a hotel

Fact 7: The Texas Rangers baseball franchise was owned by George Bush from 1989 to 1994. In 1991, a new stadium was in the process of being built and cost $191 million. The stadium was funded by a voter-approved local tax increase.

Fact 8:He recieved over half a million votes less than Al Gore but won because he recieved 271 electoral votes to Al Gore's 266.

Fact 9: When Bush took to the White House the letter W had disappeared from computer keyboards cupboards being glued shut and pornographic images placed in printers in what was allegedly an act of sabotage from the Clinton administration.

Fact 10. The W stands for Walker

Fact 11: He didn't veo anything during his first term

Fact 12: One of his most treasured items is a photo of himself and ZZ Top

Fact 13: He appointed to a senior cabinet role the first ever African-American woman

Fact 14: He was arrested on a DUI charge

Fact 15: Although several attempts were made during Bush's presidency to have him impeached, the most notable occasions occurred in June 2008 when Congressmen Dennis Kucinich and Robert Wrexler introduced 35 articles into the US House of Representatives. The 35 articles of impeachment covered a whole range of issues - including the Iraq War, which enveloped 20 of them, as well as spy-tapping in the US and global warming denials but were eventually dismissed by the Speaker. Speaker Nancy Pelosi a Democrat from California declared that impeachment was "off the table", even though the House voted 251 to 166 in favour to refer the resolution to its Judiciary Committee.

Fact 16: He has painted portrauts of world leaders sucj as Tony Blair and Vladimir Putin

Fact 17: A man from Georgia (Country) attempted to blow him up during his Presidency

Fact 18: He played Rugby Union for Yale

Fact 19: He was the first sitting U.S President to attend a papal funeral

Fact 20: He was reading a book to school children when he recieved the news of 9/11

Myth 1: George W.Bush lacks intelligence. This is an image that media and comedians seem to have portrayed in George that along with his tendency to muddle words has not done him any favors at all and use self deprecating humor but the truth is he is quite an intellegent man by no mean a genius but by the same token he is no idiot.

Myth 2: If the supreme court had not stopped the recount in Florida Bush would have lost. Not true many scholars have looked into this and came up with the answer that if the recount had gone ahead Bush would still .have won Florida and defeated Al Gore.

Barack Obama

Name: Barack Obama

Date of Birth: 4th August 1961

Place of Birth: Honolulu, Hawaii

President Number: 44

Preceded By: George W. Bush

Succeeded By: N/A

Presidential Years: 2009-present

Political Party: Democratic Party

Date of Death: N/A

Place of Death: N/A

Facts and Myths

Fact 1: He collects Spiderman comics

Fact 2: His name means "one who is blessed"

Fact 3: He has won a Grammy

Fact 4: He is left handed

Fact 5: He has red every Harry Potter book.

Fact 6: He can speak Spanish

Fact 7: He refused to watch CNN and opted for sports during his campaign

Fact 8: He broke his promise to Michelle that he would quit smoking before he ran for President.

Fact 9: While in Indonesia he had a pet Ape named Tata

Fact 10: He can bench press 200lb

Fact 11: He made $4.2m (£2.7m) in one year much of it coming from book sales.

Fact 12: He carries a tiny Madonna and child statue and a bracelet belonging to a soldier in Iraq for good luck.

Fact 13: He applied to appear in a black pin-up calendar while at Harvard but was rejected by the all-female committee

Fact 14: He plays Scrabble and Poker.

Fact 15: He took drugs as a teen including Marijuana and Cocaine

Fact 16: He only repaid his student loan after signing his book deal.

Fact 17: He has his hair cut once a week

Fact 18: He keeps on his desk a carving of a wooden hand holding an egg, a Kenyan symbol of the fragility of life.

Myth 1: Barack Hussein Obama is a muslim. While it is true his father was a muslim Barack is not he has stated he is a devout Christian

Myth 2: Barack was born in Kenya. Not true he was born in Honolulu, Hawaii

End Thoughts

Thank you for reading, I hope you enjoyed this book and maybe even found out one or two pieces of new information. Thank you.